Jackie Robinson
Hero of Baseball

Carin T. Ford

Enslow Elementary

an imprint of

Enslow Publishers, Inc.

40 Industrial Road   PO Box 38
Box 398   Aldershot
Berkeley Heights, NJ 07922   Hants GU12 6BP
USA   UK

http://www.enslow.com

Enslow Elementary, an imprint of Enslow Publishers, Inc.

Enslow Elementary® is a registered trademark of Enslow Publishers, Inc.

Library of Congress Cataloging-in-Publication Data

Ford, Carin T.
   Jackie Robinson, hero of baseball / Carin T. Ford.
      p. cm. — (Heroes of American history)
   Includes index.
   ISBN 0-7660-2600-0 (hardcover)
   1. Robinson, Jackie, 1919–1972—Juvenile literature. 2. Baseball players—United States—Biography—Juvenile literature. I. Title. II. Series.
   GV865.R6F68 2006
   796.357'092-dc22

                                    2005009501

Printed in the United States of America

10 9 8 7 6 5 4 3 2 1

To Our Readers: We have done our best to make sure all Internet Addresses in this book were active and appropriate when we went to press. However, the author and the publisher have no control over and assume no liability for the material available on those Internet sites or on other Web sites they may link to. Any comments or suggestions can be sent by e-mail to comments@enslow.com or to the address on the back cover.

Every effort has been made to locate all copyright holders of material used in this book. If any errors or omissions have occurred, corrections will be made in future editions of this book.

Illustration Credits: AP/Wide World, pp. 2, 3, 4, 12, 13, 14, 17, 18, 20, 21, 22, 24, 25, 26 (all), 27, 28 (both), 29 (both); Artville LLC, p. 7; Enslow Publishers, Inc., p. 8; Getty Images, p. 1; Library of Congress, p. 9; National Baseball Hall of Fame Library, Cooperstown, NY, pp. 6, 10; National Baseball Library (originally from *New York World-Telegram*), p. 16.

Cover Photograph: AP/Wide World (portrait); © Corel Corporation, Inc. (background).

Table of Contents

Jackie Robinson

Chapter 1

Fighting Back

When Jackie Robinson was growing up, white Americans treated black Americans badly. Jackie knew this was not right. One day, when Jackie was about eight, a white girl started making fun of him because of the color of his skin. The girl shouted at Jackie, and he shouted back. The girl's father came outside. Jackie and the man started throwing stones at each other. Finally, the girl's mother put an end to the fight.

Jackie grew up in this house on Pepper Street. Here, his mother is on the porch, and grown-up Jackie plays ball with two boys.

This would not be Jackie's only fight about being black. He did stop throwing stones. But he never stopped speaking out for the rights of African Americans. Jackie's belief in fairness would help him become one of the most important players in American baseball.

Jack Roosevelt Robinson was born on January 31, 1919, near Cairo, Georgia. His parents, Mallie and

Jerry Robinson, had five children: Edgar, Frank, Mack, Willa Mae, and baby Jackie. The family lived on a farm owned by a white farmer. Jerry worked in the fields. The farmer took most of the crops and paid Jerry only $12 a month. Jackie's family was very poor. It was a hard life.

When Jackie was six months old, his father left home and never came back. The next year, Mallie took her family across the country to Pasadena, California. They moved into a house on Pepper Street. Most of the neighbors were white. They did not want an African-American family living nearby.

Mallie got a job as a maid, but she did not earn much money. Sometimes the children had to eat bread soaked in water for dinner. Other days, they ate leftovers that Mallie brought home from work. Jackie and his brothers and sister

CALIFORNIA

• Pasadena

cut grass, shined shoes, and did other jobs to help earn money for the family.

Jackie's mother worked all day long, so the children were often on their own. Willa Mae took care of her little brother. While she was in school, Jackie played in the sandbox outside. She watched him through the classroom window.

When Jackie started school, he liked playing sports better than studying. He was good at just about every sport he tried—baseball, basketball, soccer, handball, dodgeball, even marbles.

At that time, African Americans were not allowed to eat in many restaurants. They could not sit near white people at the movies or at ball games. They could not swim together in the city swimming pool. Jackie and

Black people had to sit upstairs at this movie theater. They could not sit near white people.

his friends were angry about these rules. They started a club called the Pepper Street Gang. They stole food, threw dirt at cars, and often got into trouble with the police.

A man who worked nearby saw Jackie with the gang. He gave Jackie some advice. He told Jackie not to follow the crowd—not to lie and steal with his friends. The man said it took "courage . . . to be different." Jackie would remember those words for a long time.

Jackie at home with his mother and brother Mack.

Chapter 2

A Top Athlete

By the time Jackie was fourteen, he was known as a top athlete. "He just took up a sport and he was the best," said his brother Mack. In high school, Jackie played football, basketball, and baseball, and he ran on the track team. Then he went to Pasadena Junior College, a two-year school. People soon found out that Jackie was great at sports, especially baseball.

Jackie was a bold player who liked taking risks.

Jackie scored many touchdowns on the football field in college.

In one game, he stole second and third bases—and then stole home. In track, Jackie made a new school record for the longest broad jump. He jumped twenty-five and a half feet.

At age twenty, Jackie went to the University of California at Los Angeles. He was the first person at the school to play on four varsity teams—basketball, baseball, football, and track. For every sport he played, Jackie won an award. Many people called Jackie one of the best football players in the country.

In college, Jackie met Rachel Isum. She was studying to be a nurse. Jackie enjoyed talking to her. At first, Rachel did not like Jackie, but as she got to know him, Rachel changed her mind. The two began spending a lot of time together.

Just a few months before the end of his college years, Jackie dropped out.

Jackie was also the best player on the college basketball team.

Jackie and Rachel

Both his mother and Rachel did not want Jackie to quit school. But Jackie said it was time for him to get a job and help his mother pay her bills.

Jackie dreamed of a future in sports, but he knew that none of the major sports teams were willing to hire an African-American player. Instead, he hoped to find work as a sports coach or a gym teacher.

Chapter 3

Army Life

J ackie had a few different jobs after he left college. First he was a sports director for a few months at a camp for poor teenagers. Then he played football with a team in Hawaii. After the football season, in December 1941, he took a ship home to California. Jackie was still on the ship when the United States began to fight in World War II. This big war was already going on in Europe.

In March 1942, Jackie went to Fort Riley, Kansas, to learn how to be a soldier in the army. Even in the army, white people were treated better than blacks. Jackie wanted to become an officer, but at first he was turned down because of the color of his skin. Finally, in January 1943, Jackie was allowed to go to officers' school. As an officer, he would be in charge of a unit of African-American soldiers.

One day, on an army bus, the driver ordered Jackie to move to the back of the bus. At that time, black Americans were not allowed to sit near whites at the front of city buses. But on army buses, a new law said that blacks could sit anywhere

Jackie was in the army for three years.

African Americans had to sit in the back on this city bus.

they liked. So Jackie refused to move. The bus driver yelled at him and called the army police. Jackie was arrested, but in the end he was not punished. He had not broken the law.

In November 1944, Jackie's three years in the army were over. He heard that a baseball team called

Jackie on the Kansas City Monarchs.

the Kansas City Monarchs was looking for players, and he joined the team. The Monarchs were part of a group called the Negro Leagues. In those days, black athletes were not allowed to play on the same baseball teams as whites. So they formed the Negro Leagues.

In 1945, a baseball manager named Branch Rickey had an idea. He believed it was time for blacks and whites to play baseball together. Jackie was the player he picked to change baseball history.

Chapter 4

Crossing the Color Line

Branch Rickey was the head of the Brooklyn Dodgers baseball team in New York. He thought any good ballplayer—with any color skin— should be allowed to play major league baseball. That was a shocking idea in 1945. Baseball fans and other athletes would be very upset. Branch picked Jackie for two reasons: Jackie had talent—and he had courage. When he asked Jackie to play for him,

Branch, right, told Jackie to show everyone that he was "not only a great ballplayer but also a great gentleman."

Jackie said that he felt "thrilled, scared, and excited."

"Have you got the guts to play the game no matter what happens?" Branch asked.

"I think I can," said Jackie. Branch made Jackie promise that no matter what anyone said or did, he would not fight back.

On February 10, 1946, Jackie married Rachel. They moved to Montreal, Canada, where Jackie would be playing baseball with the Montreal Royals.

That was a minor league team owned by the Dodgers. Players often start in the minor leagues before they move up to the major leagues. Branch also knew that black people were treated better in Canada than in the United States.

The fans in Canada loved Jackie. They cheered wildly as he smashed the ball into the outfield, stole bases, and ran around the field like lightning. They did not care about his skin color. They just wanted to see a great baseball game.

Jackie's first day at practice with the Montreal Royals.

When the team traveled to cities in the United States, it was different. At the games, people yelled and booed and threw garbage at Jackie. Pitchers fired fast balls at Jackie's head to scare him. Still, Jackie kept his promise to Branch. He did not fight back. Rachel's love helped him through the worst times.

Jackie acted as if nothing bothered him, but that was not true. He often had trouble sleeping and felt too upset to eat. Yet Jackie found the courage to play his best. He won the league batting title and scored the most runs. He also helped the Royals win the minor league championship.

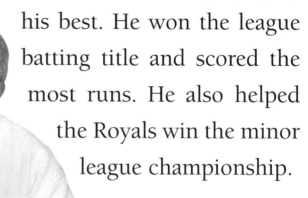

Jackie and Rachel with Jackie Jr. at home.

Chapter 5

Courage and Dignity

Jackie left Canada to play for the Brooklyn Dodgers in 1947. He was twenty-eight years old. At first, many of the Dodgers were angry. They did not want Jackie on their team, and they let him know it. Fielders from the other teams treated Jackie the worst. They kicked him or dug their spikes into him as he slid into a base.

Life in the major leagues was very hard for Jackie.

People wrote letters threatening to kill him or Rachel or kidnap Jackie Jr. They demanded that he quit the team. Sometimes when the Dodgers traveled, Jackie was not allowed to eat with his teammates or stay in the same hotels.

The other Dodgers saw how badly Jackie was treated. After a while, his teammates began to stand up for him. During one game, as the crowd shouted out insults, shortstop Pee Wee Reese walked over and put his hand on Jackie's shoulder. They talked until the crowd grew quiet. It was Pee Wee's way of showing respect for Jackie in front of everyone else.

The rest of the team began to accept Jackie.

Safe! Jackie stole home.

By the end of Jackie's first season in the major leagues, many people changed their minds. The Dodgers won the pennant for the first time in six years. More fans came to the games than ever before. Jackie had proved that he was a star athlete—an amazing batter, fielder, and runner. People also grew to admire Jackie for his courage. Jackie gave hope to millions of black people that America was changing, and their lives would be better in the future.

Off the ballfield, Jackie (1) hosted a radio show, (2) starred in a movie about his life, (3) spoke out for civil rights, and (4) often worked with young people.

Jackie played with the Dodgers for ten years. He played in six World Series. In 1955, his talent and daring on the ballfield helped the Dodgers win the World Series.

Jackie stopped playing baseball after the 1956 season. He became a vice president for the Chock Full O' Nuts company in New York. He also spent much of his time traveling around the country. He gave many speeches about fairness and equal rights for African Americans. In 1962, Jackie was elected to the National Baseball Hall of Fame.

There were many days when Jackie did not feel well. He had a serious illness called diabetes, and he was losing his eyesight. Jackie died of a

Jackie's 10 Years in the Majors	
Batting Average	.311
Total Hits	1,518
Home Runs	137
Stolen Bases	197
Runs	947
Runners Batted In (RBIs)	734

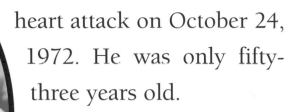

heart attack on October 24, 1972. He was only fifty-three years old.

In 1997, twenty-five years after Jackie died, all major league baseball teams agreed that no player would ever again be allowed to wear Jackie's uniform number, 42. He is the only player ever to be honored in this way.

Even when he was a young boy, Jackie Robinson stood up for his beliefs. He was a great athlete who used his talent and courage both on and off the ballfield to help make America a better country for all people.

Jackie was the first African American in the National Baseball Hall of Fame.

Timeline

1919~Born January 31, near Cairo, Georgia.

1937~Begins Pasadena Junior College.

1939~Enrolls at University of California at Los Angeles.

1942~Is in the U.S. Army.

1945~Plays for Kansas City Monarchs, a Negro League team.

1946~Marries Rachel Isum. Plays for Montreal Royals, a minor league team.

1947~Joins the Brooklyn Dodgers, a major league team.

1949~Voted Most Valuable Player in the National League.

1957~Retires from baseball.

1962~Elected to the Baseball Hall of Fame.

1972~Dies October 24.

1984~Is awarded the Presidential Medal of Freedom.

2005~Is awarded a Congressional Gold Medal.

Words to Know

batting average—How often a batter gets a hit out of all his times at bat.

major leagues—The main group of professional baseball teams in the United States.

National Baseball Hall of Fame—A museum that honors great baseball players. It is in Cooperstown, New York.

Negro Leagues—All-black leagues formed when black players were not allowed to play on major league teams.

varsity—The college sports teams that play against other schools.

World Series—The major league championship that is played by the best American League team and the best National League team.

World War II—A war fought in Europe from 1939 to 1945. The United States, Great Britain, France, and the Soviet Union defeated Germany, Italy, and Japan.

Learn More

Books

Brown, Jonatha A. *Jackie Robinson*. Milwaukee, Wisc.: Weekly Reader Learning Library, 2005.

McLeese, Don. *Jackie Robinson*. Vero Beach, Fla.: Rourke, 2003.

Schaefer, Lola M. *Jackie Robinson*. Mankato, Minn.: Pebble Books, 2003.

Internet Addresses

Baseball and Jackie Robinson.
 <http://lcweb2.loc.gov/ammem/collections/ robinson/>

National Baseball Hall of Fame: Jackie Robinson.
 <http://www.baseballhalloffame.org>
 Type "Jackie Robinson" into the SEARCH box. Then click on the link called "Jackie Robinson / National Baseball Hall of Fame."

Index